JOZEF ISRAËLS

BY

J. ERNEST PHYTHIAN

AUTHOR OF "FIFTY YEARS OF MODERN PAINTING," "TURNER"
"WATTS," "MILLAIS," "BURNE-JONES," ETC.

LONDON
GEORGE ALLEN & COMPANY, LTD.
44 & 45 RATHBONE PLACE
1912

LIST OF ILLUSTRATIONS

JOZEF ISRAËLS

The pictures marked * are in the Rijksmuseum at Amsterdam ; those marked † are in the Stedelijkmuseum at Amsterdam.

FAGGOT GATHERERS

By kind permission of Messrs. Wallis & Son

JOZEF ISRAËLS

THE painter whose work is discussed in the following pages had the distinction of being a leader in a movement that took the art of his country back to a vivid and inspiring interpretation of contemporary life, and of the natural world in which that life was lived, from which it had long departed to give instead pictures of mythological and historical subjects that were supposed to have both in their art and in their subjects an importance that records of immediate, ordinary happenings could not have. Dutch painting had been led to make this change by French influence at the close of the seventeenth century, after giving, during that century, the first example of the devotion of a national art to a record of contemporary life, and of the country in which the nation had its home.

A

JOZEF ISRAËLS

In the Middle Ages art was mainly in the service of the Church; and it was only so far as they incidentally fitted in with the representation of sacred subjects that ordinary people and things received any attention. The Renaissance, the awakening of men's minds to the value of pre-Christian literature and art, added, as another province of art, the interpretation of pre-Christian mythology. It also gradually led to a wider outlook upon life and nature. Portrait painting became common. Landscape was painted alone, for its own sake, and not as a mere setting for figures. Lords and ladies were relieved from attendance on the Virgin and saints, and had their own doings recorded; and in time the common people received their share of attention.

These changes were first fully worked out in Holland, which, by the beginning of the seventeenth century, had virtually thrown off, after a long and heroic struggle, the double yoke, ecclesiastical and civil, of Spain, and had established a republic, and the right freely to worship according to the tenets of Protestant belief. The foundations had also been laid of a commercial

2

prosperity that went on steadily expanding, along with a vigorous intellectual life, in which art, in particular the art of painting, had a full share.

Protestantism closed to the painters of Holland the whole great cycle of subjects which had not so much been at the disposal of, as been imposed upon, the artists of the time when the Catholic Church ruled supreme, and had been put to such splendid use. It might have been expected that the Dutch would ask their painters to celebrate the victories that had won for them their freedom. But they did not. What was asked was a record of themselves and their wives and children, of their daily life, of the look of their towns, their country, their sea-coast. What Dutch life was in the seventeenth century can be better realised, in some ways at least, by looking at the contemporary pictures of it than by reading books about it. The country and the towns retain sufficient of their old character, and so do the people in many respects, to assure us, when compared with the old pictures, that the painters' record is a true one. Not that it is merely record. It is record in terms of art. The Dutch painters of the seventeenth century were excel-

JOZEF ISRAËLS

lent craftsmen, exhibiting varied styles of work.
There were among them fine colourists, true
musicians in colour; their pictures were skilfully
composed; and they included one of the
very greatest masters of art, Rembrandt. It
is not to our purpose to discuss the work of
these painters in any detail here. It is enough
to say that among them they gave a full record
of contemporary life. Adrien Brauwer, Adrien
and Isaac van Ostade, and Jan Steen took the
peasantry for their subject, and cannot be accused
of giving them credit for more refinement than
they possessed. Jan Steen also joined such
painters as Terborch and Vermeer of Delft—two
fine colourists—Metsu, Gerard Dou, and Pieter
de Hooch—a student of effects of light to whom
we shall have to refer again—in recording the
look and habits of the commercial and ruling
class. The portrait painters, with Rembrandt
facile princeps among them, are legion; they include such opposites as the brilliant Frans Hals
and the plodding Van der Helst. The sea-board,
the far-reaching prospects inland over the level
country from the dunes, the well-tilled fields, the
woodlands, the canals, the picturesque towns, and

4

the great expanse of sky over all, inspired a numerous company of landscape painters, including that great master Jacob Ruysdael, and, among the rest, Hobbema, Van der Neer, De Koninck, Albert Cuyp, the Van der Velde family, and Backhuysen. It was Holland and its people, almost exclusively, that these painters took for their subject. They restricted themselves, or, rather, the existing conditions restricted them, to first-hand interpretation of life and nature.

But about the end of the century a change came. The great epoch in Dutch history was over. As the national force and prosperity declined, art declined with it; losing its vitality, it became feeble and imitative merely; and in the early part of the nineteenth century it had made no recovery, but was merely echoing first the Classicism and then the Romanticism of French art.

Israëls thought that this change had been a lamentable one for the art of his country. In the course of an essay written for the volume on Rembrandt in Messrs. Jack's "Masterpieces in Colour" series, he says that even in Rembrandt's lifetime there were people who condemned him

5

JOZEF ISRAËLS

" because he refused to follow in the footsteps of
the old Italian painters, because he persisted in
painting nature as he saw it"; and he refers to
the change of ideas in the Dutch mind as to
art and literature that was taking place before
Rembrandt died, a morbid taste arising for everything classical, and says that he is filled with
disgust when in the prose and poetry of the time
he finds allusions to Greek mythology that are
strangely out of place under our northern sky.

We can hardly forbid the northern peoples to
take interest in the gods of southern climes, or
say that the interest must not reveal itself in art
and literature ; and we have no need to consider
whether or not the interest taken in these subjects
by the Dutch artists was wholly a morbid one. It
is at least arguable that, after long confining themselves to one kind of subject, art and literature
may by inward compulsion have to make a
change—even if, as we say, the change be for
the worse. Such questions as these we need not
discuss, but can content ourselves with simply
stating that there was a return to mythological
subjects, and that, later again, when the time was
ripe, there was a return to contemporary life as

6

the main subject for art, and that Israëls was a leader, we may even say the leader, in directing Dutch art back to the path it had trodden in the seventeenth century. In the following pages we shall not only consider his art, but shall briefly take note of the art of some of his contemporaries who made common cause with him.

Jozef Israëls was born at Groningen, in North Holland, on the 27th of January 1824. One of his pictures, reproduced in this book, is called *A Son of the Old Folk*, and to the Old Folk, the Jewish race, Israëls himself belonged. His father carried on a small banking business at Groningen, a minor commercial town, and the son, when he left school, naturally, until his strong individual bent showed itself, prepared to follow the paternal occupation. At one time he had thought of becoming a rabbi, and studied the Hebrew language and the Talmud. This intention, however, was abandoned; but the fact that at one time it possessed him is instructive in view of the generally serious treatment of human life in his pictures. "Man's mortality," in Wordsworth's phrase, was never far absent from his thought; yet things did not perhaps take quite as "sober colouring" with him as some who have written about him have seemed to think. He never lost sympathy with his own people. When, late in life, he made a journey to Spain, to which we shall refer later, and at Avignon, on the return homewards, he saw a synagogue, it awakened in him the reflection that there some of his sorely persecuted kinsmen had found a resting-place, and that, amid many churches and monasteries erected for Gentile worship, a company of the Chosen People had its house of prayer.

The young Israëls was not destined to be either banker or rabbi. Art began to claim him for its own ; and, happily, his parents were willing that he should respond to what clearly declared itself to be an imperative call. His systematic instruction in art did not begin until he was about twenty years old, when he went to Amsterdam, and entered the studio of Jan Kruseman, then one of the most reputed painters of historical pictures and portraits. In his notes on the art of Rembrandt, in the little volume already mentioned, Israëls has given incidentally an instructive account of an experience of his student-days. He wished to copy some of the portraits painted

JOZEF ISRAËLS

by his master, with their pink flesh-tints, and
carefully executed draperies set off by a back-
ground of dark red velvet. But the master knew
of greater masters than himself, and sent the
youth to the Trippenhuis, an old mansion, used
as an art gallery, in which were exhibited pictures
by the old Dutch masters, now to be seen in the
great Rijksmuseum. But as our own Sir Joshua
Reynolds, when he went to Italy, found himself
unable at first to appreciate the works of the
great Italian masters, so the young Israëls found
himself unable to appreciate those of the great
Dutch painters of the seventeenth century, the
works of his own older contemporaries being much
more to his liking. Smooth and delicate painting
was what he admired, and it was only after long
practice, in the open air and in the studio, that he
came to give the first place to truth of light and
shade, of relief and of the attitude, movement,
and gesture of figures : the things that, in after
years, became almost the be-all and the end-all of
his art. Having made this advance, the work
of the old masters began to give him pleasure ;
he saw that a simple subject could be dignified
by manner of treatment ; he copied from Gerard

JOZEF ISRAËLS

Dou and Van der Helst ; and at last found his way to Rembrandt. He copied the head of the man in the left-hand corner of *The Syndics*, studied carefully this picture and *The Night-Watch*, and then had eyes for nothing but Rembrandt, finding his chief qualities to be freedom and exuberance, which were conspicuously absent, indeed positively forbidden, in his master, Kruseman's studio. Then he found Rembrandt's etchings in the print-room of the Trippenhuis, and also his drawings, and was amazed by their expressiveness : not a fragment of line but had its individual meaning. Walking homewards after these studies at the Trippenhuis, through the Hoog Straat and St. Anthony's Breestraat to where he lived, close to Rembrandt's house in the Joden Breestraat, he saw Rembrandt's people and pictures all the way.

But although his eyes were thus opened by Rembrandt to the significance, and to the value for art, of the familiar city streets and the people who crowded them, he did not at once break away from contemporary theory and practice to follow Rembrandt in his first-hand interpretation of life. Kruseman, though he could send his pupil to

10

JOZEF ISRAËLS

study at the Trippenhuis, was none the less an academic painter, and Israëls had no other immediate thought than to follow his instruction, and so prepare himself to paint the kind of picture then in vogue.

In 1845 he went to Paris, and remained there for about three years. Here he placed himself under Picot, a pupil of Jacques Louis David, the leader of the French classical school, which, slavishly worshipping all things Greek, modelled its painting on Greek sculpture, in default of any adequate knowledge of how the Greeks painted. From Picot he passed to Paul Delaroche; hence there is little wonder that what he had learned from Rembrandt remained unapplied, and that the pictures he exhibited after his return to Holland in 1848 were of historical subjects such as *Hamlet and his Mother* and *Prince Maurice of Nassau beside the Body of his Father*, which we might well expect from the pupil of the painter of *The Princes in the Tower*, *The Death of Queen Elizabeth*, and *The Murder of the Duke of Guise in the Castle of Blois.*

The awakening, however, was not to be long delayed. A serious illness sent him to the fishing village of Zandvoort, near Haarlem, to recruit his health ; and here he found the inspiration that was to suffice for the work of a long life.

Not many people, probably, would suppose the coast of Holland to be capable of inspiring an artist. Almost as if their edges had been drawn with a ruler, the breakers, the belt of utterly stone-less, grey-brown sand, and the dunes, stretch north and south past Zandvoort until they fade in the distance. To the fishing village of Israëls' early years there has now been added a conventional seaside resort. Writing home from Blackpool, when he was a boy, Burne-Jones said that he did not see why the place should have such a name, since most of the houses were white—they were fishermen's cottages. Israëls, at Zandvoort, made his home in the house of a ship's carpenter. The place and the people together speedily appealed to him as subject-matter enough for his art; and, though he did not wholly abandon his-torical painting, the life and surroundings of the Dutch fisher-folk and peasantry, as he intimately knew them through living amongst them, hence-forth, with an approach to exclusiveness that might lead the superficial observer of his work to be ready to accuse it of monotony, absorbed his interest.

It is probable that the interval between his recognition, under the influence of Rembrandt, of the pictorial value of contemporary life, and his actual giving of himself to its interpretation, was of no little advantage to him. It saved him from any risk of being a mere imitator of Rembrandt. The influence that had lain dormant for years now leaped into activity under an impulse derived, not from art, but from life and from nature. He was brought right up against the fundamental simplicities of life. At Zandvoort there was no Trippenhuis ; there were no exhibitions of modern paintings ; there were no studios and studio-talk, yet this was the place he found to be, for him, as an artist, holy ground. We may liken him to the apostle, taught in a vision that nothing is common or unclean. He saw that the toilers by and on the sea, and their wives and children, with surroundings of sand-dunes and far-stretching ocean, grey under grey, and bright under sunny skies, were excellent material for art. We will put it that way first. Good pictures were to be made from them—good in light and tone and colour. Go where he might, he would find nothing better for his purpose. But was there enough of story, incident, subject ? There were the seven ages of man—and death at the finish. Were not these subject enough ? At any rate he found them so. They were enough, with the painting of relatively a few portraits, and still fewer historical—mainly Old Testament subjects —to satisfy him for the work of his life. Similarly the life of the peasantry sufficed for the life-work of Jean François Millet, with whom Israëls is often compared. How far the comparison can legitimately be carried, we shall consider later. In our own country, and among our contemporaries, we may think of Mr. George Clausen's faithfulness to the peasantry and landscape of Essex, and of Mr. Edward Stott's to those of Sussex.

It must have been with a great joy that Israëls found what the working-folk could be to him. He was not one of them ; it was not with him as with Millet, who said that he was at home only with the peasantry to whom he belonged. But in the deepest sense Israëls was one with the poor of his own land ; he was a man of large sympathy with his kind ; and the

CHILDREN OF THE SEA

JOZEF ISRAËLS

Dutch fisher-folk, in their cottages among the sand-dunes, with the ocean beyond and the sky above, were not only pictorial, they were intensely human.

Before we follow any further the progress of Israëls' art, it will be useful if we can learn something more about the man himself; and this we shall best do by turning to an account he wrote and published of a journey to Spain, undertaken in 1898, when he was seventy-four years of age. It might seem as if we should get from this an idea of him only when he was an old man; but there is such a naïve boyishness about the narrative, and about the zest with which he flung himself into the enjoyment of new experiences, as to convince us that he carried into old age the freshness of youth, and that, knowing him as he was at seventy-four, we know him as he was through all his working life.

It is with the artist that we are concerned, and with the man in so far as what we can know of him will help us better to appreciate his art. And do we not understand better how Dutch art in general, and that of Israëls in particular, came to be what it is, when he says, observing how the cathedral at Burgos dominates and belittles the town, that it was built at a time when the Church counted for everything and humanity for nothing? The papal palace at Avignon calls from him the remark that at the time it was built, what we call humanity was not known. When his son—who, and a young literary friend, were his fellow-travellers—helps an acolyte in the cathedral at Barcelona to move things too heavy for the boy to move unaided, he comments on this co-operation of Jew and Catholic, and on the absurdity of quarrelling about the service of a Being of whom mortals know so little.

At the Prado, he feels that the pictures of Madonnas, saints, and angels, by their very number, lose their individual value; but he shows his capacity and willingness to see the spiritual worth of other religious traditions than those in which he has been nurtured when he says that if Christian subjects were a new idea, a single picture of Mary, disconsolate at the foot of the cross, with her noble son looking down upon her, would kill every surrounding

16

JOZEF ISRAËLS

picture. The triumph of Velasquez at the Prado is emphasised, he notes, by the contrast between the subject-matter of most of his pictures and that of so many of their neighbours.

We might paraphrase an old proverb, and say that the artist's eye is subdued to what he paints, when we read of an incident that occurred during a stroll through Toledo. He was attracted by the sound of a woman singing to a crying child. Through a grated window he saw a young mother, with a rose in her black hair, a yellow, flowered handkerchief over her bosom, and a grey petticoat. A child in her arms sobbed as she sang to it, tapping an accompaniment on the grating with her fan. Concert and picture in one, says the artist. Soon the father, a pedlar, comes along, singing; the mother holds the child to the grating to be kissed; now the father is in the room with the child in his arms, while the mother prepares a simple meal.

Another incident, at Algeciras, is amusingly characteristic of Israëls. He stops to look at a woman, with a child in her arms, gazing out to sea. He is rebuked by his travelling-companions, who tell him that train-time is near, and, further,

C   17

that he has often seen that kind of thing at home. He cannot deny it; he has seen and painted such an incident not once nor twice. The figures are different in appearance and surroundings; but essentially, anywhere, a mother with her child, looking out to sea, is the same. Such a scene is a phrase in the still, sad music of humanity.

A visitor to his studio once found him sitting, doing nothing, at an hour when he was usually at work. "How is this?" asked the visitor. "Oh," replied the painter, "I am thinking of the subjects I must not paint." Yet, although he kept his own practice within narrow limits, he was by no means blind to the paintable quality of subjects he did not attempt. He saw in Spain many that he could portion out to other painters. A clerical librarian at Madrid, whose bald skull shone in the sunlight, would have suited the gloomy Ribera. A quack doctor at Barcelona, bandaging a porter's injured foot, with a crowd of children watching him, would have been just the thing for Jan Steen; a night-porter at a hotel, asleep amid a pile of boxes, in a cavernous apartment lighted only by a candle, was a subject for Rembrandt. When a landing-boat comes to

take passengers off the steamer by which he is
crossing to Tangier, her. dusky crew in white
turbans, her brilliantly-hued carpets and cushions,
with the intense blue of the sea around them,
present a many-coloured *tableau vivant*, that calls
to mind Decamps, Delacroix, Rubens, Ribera,
and many other masters of the brush.

Always he sees as an artist, while he feels as a
man. A portly ecclesiastic passes by, big nosed,
wide mouthed, flabby cheeked, double chinned.
How delightful it would be to paint him! But
such a proposal would have been scorned by the
church dignitary. He could only be regretfully
followed with the eye : an escaped quarry!
Whereupon the painter laments, as a drawback
to his calling, that so often something is seen
only to disappear before it can be adequately
observed.

The story of this Spanish journey from beginning to end is a series of pictures, some with a
subject, some without. The faded splendour of
the famous mosque at Cordova fills him and his
travelling-companions with melancholy. But they
step out into the sunshine, see a palm-tree in the
middle of the sandy road, and a brown boy with

a stick tending his black goats. Cheerfulness is
at once restored, and the artist concludes that
there is a charm about everyday life that lifts
it far above the noblest works of art.

Just after he has seen the mother and child at
Toledo, he comes across a tall peasant in a straw
hat and dark blue coat driving a grey donkey
which carries a pannier containing an almost
naked child with an apple in its hand. A complete picture, but, alas! no chance to paint it.
Only a sketch-book note of it is possible on
returning to the hotel.

At Seville, the fine shops and the cafés have
no attraction for him. He hurries away to the
slums. An open door, a light within, the sound
of a Spanish barrel-organ like to that of a com-
bination of guitar and concertina, at each side of
the door a statue of the Blessed Virgin, decorated
with flowers and leaves and lighted by candles;
inside, under the star-lit sky, a space illuminated
with variously-coloured paper lanterns; dancing,
to watch which chairs are placed for himself and
his companions, the visit ending in the fair
dancers and their swains being treated to wine
at the strangers' expense: here is material for a

A FRUGAL MEAL.

picture in impressionist genre, or for a kaleido-scopic futurist venture.

In a church at Barcelona he chances upon a widely different scene. The church is empty. He is turning to leave it; when three tall women, dressed in black, enter, pass along as if they do not see him, and kneel just before him in front of a statue of the Blessed Virgin fixed against a pillar. The tallest of the three is in the centre; she is black-haired and pallid; the other two throw their arms about her neck. She takes out a book of prayer and reads aloud; the others, with bowed heads, listen, praying with her. A sculptor would have been inspired by this group, thinks the painter; it is so harmonious in its forms, and so nobly expressive of grief.

To his judgment on the relative merits of the art of Velasquez and that of Rembrandt we shall refer later; meanwhile we are not surprised that at Seville he cannot bring himself to like the art of Murillo; it is too sweet, smooth, suave in colour and form. He sets over against it the regal manner of Velasquez and the rugged force of Ribera. Suddenly he calls his companions to come and look at a Morales, an ugly grey-green

JOZEF ISRAËLS

picture—a Pietà, Mary with emaciated face looking down on the body of her Son, which lies in her lap. It nobly expresses the great tragedy. It has the simple seriousness that Murillo lacks, and none of the pompous artificiality that marks his work. It is a picture that the artist would like to have in his studio, face to the wall, to be looked at only when he is weary of the outside world and in the mood to reflect on sorrow lifted to the high, mysterious level of poetry. He thinks that pictures are too much used as mere furniture for churches and public and private buildings ; and, indeed, the great painting deserves to be treated as an end in itself.

This Spanish journey found Israëls the subject of one of the finest of his pictures ; one also, that, together with the incident now to be related, reveals to us more clearly than perhaps any other the intense humanity of the painter.

He often met with his co-religionists in Spain. Where, one might ask, are they not to be met? An Englishman was surprised once to hear a merchant at Constantinople speaking Spanish. In answer to his request for an

22

explanation, the merchant told him that he was the descendant of a Jew who was banished from Spain in the sixteenth century, and that the family had never ceased to use the Spanish tongue. At Tangier, also, Israëls came across a fellow-Jew under the following circumstances. He was filled with curiosity to see the interior of one of the great, square, stone blocks of dwellings that make up so much of the town. He was warned that it was dangerous to enter them, and that there was nothing unusual to be seen, even if he were granted admission. Who has not felt the fascination of a strange type of building, and been possessed by the idea that it must contain curious if not wonderful things? This old man of seventy-four was not too old for such youthful imaginings. He ventured into the courtyard of one of the blocks, in which a woman was drawing water from a well. Then he summoned more courage, and climbed a dark stone staircase, on which he met a woman carrying a pitcher, passed her, and reached the top of the stair, where a swaying curtain made it possible for him both to see into a room and to be seen from it. He did not dare to enter, and was surprised to hear a man's voice asking, in Hebrew : " What do you want here ? " He replied, also in Hebrew : " The Lord be with you, the Lord bless you ; I am a Jew from Holland." His questioner asked where Holland was ; and Israëls, not very proficient in Hebrew, had some difficulty in making the necessary explanation. Meanwhile, he had entered a room, into the darkness of which light pierced only through one narrow window against which was a trestle table, where an old Jewish scribe, with long white beard, large hooked nose, and bald head covered by a black cap, was writing on parchment. At his side was a pair of crutches. Not even a rough sketch could be ventured ; but the subject this time was too good to lose ; one was made afterwards, and an oil painting followed when he had returned home. He had to look at and admire the scribe's penmanship, and watch him write. Then they went out together on to the flat roof, and sat on mats, looking out over Tangier and the distant hills and sea. When he was going away, the old man put his hand on his head and said : " The Lord bless and protect you." Well might Israëls say that he felt as if he were in a

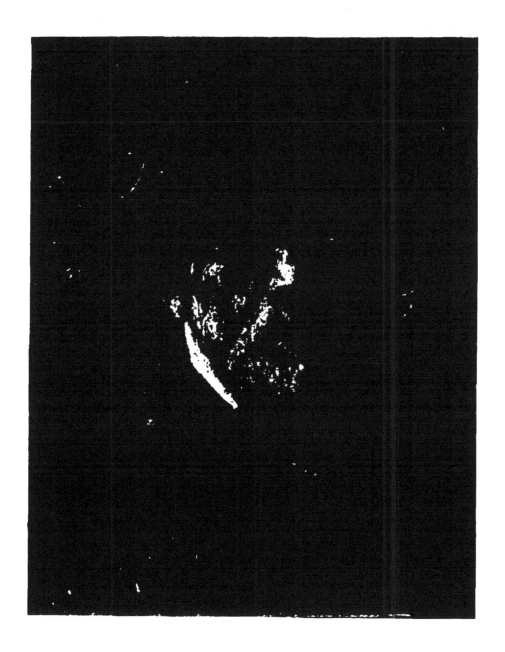

PORTRAIT OF JOZEF ISRAËLS

world he had seen in a dream. His curiosity was fully rewarded.

The reader may be recommended to read Israëls' account of this Spanish journey, of which an English translation by A. Teixeira de Mattos has been published by Mr. Nimmo. We have here gathered from it enough to make the painter more familiarly known to us, in particular, as a keen and sympathetic observer of his fellow-men; towards which entirely wholesome, and, for an artist, fruitful quality, we have seen that he owed an early stimulus to Rembrandt, and a later one, determining what his life-work should be, to the fisher-folk of Zandvoort.

Two things impress us as we read these stories of travel: the human fellow-feeling and the swift perception of the pictorial value of a scene. If we could trust the painter's own diagnosis of the motives that influenced him in his work, we might have to attach but little importance to the human sympathy. In the course of a speech made by him at a dinner given in his honour at Scheveningen, Israëls said: " I did what I could not help doing, and my sole merit is perhaps that I have let myself be guided by my conviction of what I thought beautiful. It is very gratifying to see that an idea which one has painted so strikes the heart of the spectator, that he, forgetting the art of painting, simply sees the poet in the picture. But as for me, I only painted such pictures—for example, those which are called sad and pathetic in subject—because I found in them occasion for applying the lines and the colours by which I was possessed—Heine would say : by which I was bewitched. And as regards the public—I never could stop to ask whether what I was going to do would appeal to it ; but, nevertheless, I am very thankful that there are many to whom in the end it really did appeal."

It is very difficult, surely almost impossible, to accept this statement. Can we believe that the artist, who saw in the three ladies in the church at Barcelona not merely a beautiful sculpturesque group, but also a noble expression of grief, himself painted sad and pathetic subjects merely because they gave him beautiful line and colour ? Let us take three of his early pictures, *The Way through the Churchyard*, *After the Storm*, and *The Drowned Fisherman*, all reproduced in this volume (pp. 11, 8, and 4). The pathetic incidents in these pictures, the fisherman's anguished face, and his boy's look of intense sympathy, the anxious watch seawards from the cottage door, the varying expressions of grief and sympathy as the body of the fisherman is being carried across the dunes to his village home, all these things are utterly irrelevant to considerations merely of line and colour; and the painter could not possibly have put them on the canvas without, not merely thinking of them, but sympathetically experiencing them. And while it would rob the pathos of all sincerity if we could think of it as simply calculated to attract public interest, the assertion that he never stopped to think of the public, never considered whether or not his pictures would awaken in others the emotion he had felt, is something we do not wish to believe, and will, indeed, absolutely refuse to believe.

To maintain this position we have no need to accuse Israëls of insincerity; all that we have to do is to credit him with modesty. He did not wish to make parade of his human sympathy. It may well be also that, even while painting his pictures, and much more as he looked back on his life-work, he was conscious rather of the artistic problems they presented to him than of the emotion expressed in them. We may allow for the sub-conscious; or we may say there is a sense in which his right hand did not know what his left hand was doing. It may be also that he oftener heard his pictures praised for their pathetic subjects than for their art, and that he was wishful as artist to redress the balance. There may have been a justifiable pride as well as a fine modesty; he knew his work to have a quality that too often went unrecognised. We will think otherwise of him than he might appear to wish us to think; we will say that while he did one thing he did not leave another undone—that if he never forgot what was required of him as an artist, he also never ceased from active sympathy with his fellows, though he did not lower its quality by telling himself that he possessed it. We have the testimony of those who knew him through the greater part of his life that he was a kind-hearted man, and we want such pictures as he painted to be painted by such an one.

We must now return to Israëls as a young man, seeking health at Zandvoort, and finding there more than health : a life-work.

JOZEF ISRAËLS

He was far from having reached his full development as an artist when he turned from historical subjects to the fisher-folk and the peasants. He had yet to pass in his own practice from what he had learned in Kruseman's studio, and in Paris, to what he had learned at the Trippenhuis. His early pictures, after what we may call his conversion—those dating in the fifties and the sixties—are hard in their draughtsmanship, and are lacking in atmosphere, and not merely in movement but in the possibility of movement. The lights are so many definite patches amid the shade, and the colour is in hard-edged blocks. The composition also is formal, at times almost symmetrical. The result is that the pictures have a fixed, set look, more so even than many of those of the seventeenth century masters. But the handling gradually became looser, and the composition less formal, with resultant increase in the sense of atmosphere and movement, and all that we include under the term life. In the earlier pictures we suspect the people of having been carefully grouped by the artist; in the later ones we seem to have chanced to see them, as

JOZEF ISRAËLS

Israëls himself tells us he chanced upon paintable subjects in Spain, on the shore or in the fields, or to have opened the cottage door—we can hardly understand that we are not intruding—and found them engaged in their household work, tending their children, or mourning their dead, and wholly unaware of our presence.

The method of treating colour also has entirely changed. Herr Meier-Graeffe contemptuously dismisses Israëls' colour as brown sauce. Nothing could be more unjust. So far from this, what we see, and feel, in picture after picture, is play of purple, blue, green and grey, so subtilely modulated that there are no definite patches of colour, but vibrating tints combining into a pearly tone. There are no longer, also, patches of light detaching themselves sharply from the rest of the picture when we stand back a short distance from it, but, instead, there is infinitely varied interplay of light and shade. In these qualities, the later works of Israëls are in marked contrast from those of the Dutch masters of the seventeenth century, with the exception of those of Rembrandt and his followers, and even here the sense of movement is not as strong. We

30

should be much surprised if anybody moved in a picture by even De Hooch or Vermeer of Delft, much more in one by Gerard Dou or Van Mieris; we are surprised that the people in Israëls' pictures remain still; we watch to see them finish what they are doing and turn to something else.

Is there any human work that has not the defects of its qualities? This is the justification for the saying that it takes all kinds to make a world. "I like this picture better than that one," said a visitor to an art gallery; "there is more detail in it." Those who must have detail will not care for Israëls' later pictures. They can find what they want in the work of not a few of his predecessors and contemporaries, and in his own earlier work, but they will not find there an almost illusive sense of life, of light, of atmosphere and of movement.

In the account that he gave of his art at the congratulatory dinner already mentioned, Israëls spoke of the lines and colours by which he was bewitched. The words do not seem happily chosen. Perhaps to have endeavoured to express himself more accurately would have been too pedantic for the occasion. Or it may be that we have not a verbatim report of what he said. Anyhow, Israëls' work, particularly his later work, does not suggest bewitchment by lines. Doubtless he was sensitive to beauty of line, but his art is not based upon line as was, say, Florentine art as compared with the colour basis of Venetian art, or the art of Ingres as compared with that of Delacroix—Ingres is reported to have said "Take care of the line, and the colour will take care of itself"—or, in our own country, we may contrast the art of Leighton with that of Watts. It is not especially beauty of line for which we admire the art of Israëls' great predecessor, Rembrandt; and though line inevitably plays its part in every picture, in the works of Israëls it is a subordinate one.

Nor would one single out the colour of Israëls' pictures for final emphasis. Light and atmosphere are here of first and last importance; then, as means to these ends, but with its own delightfulness, beautiful variation of tones in a limited range of colour. Of line we think hardly at all; of colour certainly a good

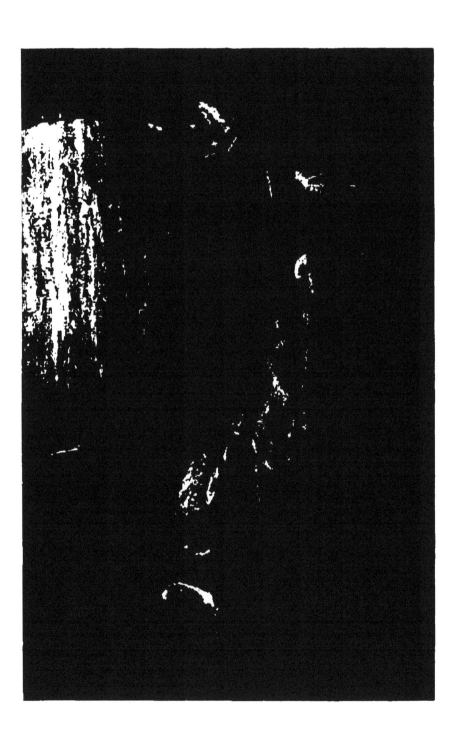

JOZEF ISRAËLS

deal, but only secondarily to the qualities first mentioned.

He plays with light and atmosphere and colour-tones, visible music which is delightful in itself. Modulation is a beautiful word that signifies beautiful things : easy, gradual changes that cause no shock to us, but give us the pleasure of variety, in what we particularly call music, through waves that reach the brain through the ear, as in other arts through the eye; and the pleasure is increased if the changes be many and intricate without being confused, so that we say we feel them rather than distinguishingly hear or see each of them. It is such feeling that is evoked by Israëls' art, especially in his later pictures. There are pleasantly modulated tones, and they have the additional, infinitely enjoyable quality of more than half deceiving us into the feeling that we actually see the play of light in an atmosphere that we could breathe. Forms are made indistinct by the light as they are in nature. There is a feeling of vibration. Nothing seems fixed. There is expression, the suggestion not the exact realisation of form, the spirit not the letter. It is so also with the

E

33

figures; they become expression rather than form, so that, represented as in movement we think of them as moving, not as merely being in the attitude of people who move; represented as talking, we think that we are listening to them; quiet, we fancy that we are following their thoughts. In one word, they live.

Israëls worked in water-colour as freely as in oil, and in both media he entirely subordinated the means to the end. We do not look at his "paint" for its own sake, for such a beauty of surface, or such skilful delineation of objects and textures as we get in the works of the old Dutch masters. His friend Jan Veth speaks of him as "fumbling in a surface of paint, feeling after the mystery of life that speaks in the outward form of things." "His figures must breathe and live," says the same writer, a fellow-painter, be it noted. On the same good authority we learn that Israëls "did not care for, could see nothing in, Japanese prints"; a failure to appreciate what is, in its way, as fine art as is, in its way, what he himself did. Yet we are hardly surprised at this limitation of his outlook. The Japanese print had aims widely different from his. It does not give the

JOZEF ISRAËLS

semblance of life. Expressive as its figures are, the last thing we expect of them is that they shall seem to live and breathe.

Jan Veth's word "fumbling" seems as if it must imply an adverse criticism. But the context shows that this is not the way in which it is used. For the fumbling is not that of incompetence, but of knowledge, acquired by experience, of the best means to an end. There is no fumbling in *The Way through the Churchyard*, or in that example of his early smooth prettiness, *The Faggot Gatherers* (p. 1). But the figures in these pictures do not live and breathe as do those in the later ones. It is this method of painting, affording no enjoyment of immediate effect as the decoration of a surface, that gives the work of Israëls a value different from that of such a painter of light as De Hooch. Subtle and beautiful as are the earlier painter's effects of light, they seem fixed for ever on the canvas, without possibility of change. In Israëls' pictures we feel that the light may increase or lessen ; that, as the workers return home through the fields, or as the weary watchers sit by the bedside of the dying, the day will slowly pass into

35

JOZEF ISRAËLS

dark. We can even fancy that change is occurring, that here the scene is lightened and there goes dull, as the clouds discover or shut out the sun.

It should at least be mentioned that Israëls used the etching-needle as well as the brush, and was, indeed, a master of this means of expression, which was admirably adapted to the rendering of the subjects that he made peculiarly his own.

Israëls' portrait painting passed through the same changes as his treatment of genre subjects. Early portraits by him are exceedingly hard. Then the handling gets gradually looser, until we have finally strokes of the brush that seem to go hither and thither at haphazard, and we wonder, when we step back from the picture, to find that they translate themselves into features and flesh-tones, and, of more importance than these, into expression which carries conviction that character has been truly interpreted.

In the Municipal Museum at The Hague there are two presentation portraits, one by Roelofs, the other by Israëls. They were painted at the same time, and were both unveiled before a company assembled to witness the ceremony. Roelofs'

JOZEF ISRAËLS

sitter, Stroebel, is well groomed ; Israëls' sitter, the artist Josselin de Jong, is in work-a-day clothes and flannel shirt ; his hair is unkempt, and he has a thoughtful, distraught expression. The wife of the latter said to one who sat beside her at the ceremony : "That is not my husband."   "O yes, madam, it is," was the reply, " but not your husband when you have seen that he is properly dressed and made presentable for some private or public function. It is your husband as he looks when he is thinking and feeling intensely, when he is doing the work for which he is now being honoured, when he is most himself."

This is the character of all Israëls' portraits. We see it in those reproduced in this volume, in the one of himself at page 24, and that of Veltman the dramatist at page 17. The summary handling of his own portrait is clearly seen in the illustration. A number of hasty brush-strokes result in the face of an old man emerging from the shade of a slouch hat ; a heavy overcoat, thrown open, hangs loosely about the shoulders. We are arrested by a serious, almost sad expression, and a keen, scrutinising look which might imply a power to penetrate beneath the surface, to see to the heart of any person upon whom it was fixed. We might well feel uncomfortable under it, were we conscious of any weakness; for the grave earnestness of the face suggests no mean standard of judgment.

The portrait of Veltman is only less loose in the handling. Sadness, almost pain, is stamped on the face. It seems to ask for sympathy. The look here is not a keen scrutiny of what is actually visible; but the far-away, introspective look of one who is calling up the unseen.

There were several portraits by Israëls in the memorial exhibition of his works held at The Hague towards the end of 1911. One of an old Jew, *A Man of the Ancient Race*, wore an exquisitely quizzical expression. In another, *Head of an Old Man*, thoughtfulness and humour were mingled. In a third portrait of an old man, a whimsical fancy seemed to be sending a fleeting expression over the face. Portraits of Herr Helwig, Jacob Stedel, and of the artist J. H. Weissenbruch—in his shirt-sleeves, smoking a pipe, and looking alert and eager—all showed grasp of essentials and indifference to irrelevant detail. In another, the brush-work was of the

JOZEF ISRAËLS

swiftest, and, closely examined, seemed utterly aimless in direction, yet the result was good modelling and convincing expression.

A portrait of a young woman was a study of a smile passing over the face of one who dreamed by day. One portrait was so treated as to become a subject-picture, and bore the title *Faith's Trustfulness*. It showed a woman with clasped hands, looking upwards with an arrestingly earnest expression. This picture alone would suffice to make us reject Israëls' assertion, previously quoted, that line and colour, alone, not emotional interest, governed the choice of his subjects.

He did not paint closely from the sitter. Usually he only made sketches; and much of the best work on his portraits was done when the sittings were over. They were not mere likenesses; they recorded the main facts of appearance, perhaps; but essentially they were interpretations: records of the impression the sitters had made on the painter.

Israëls' undoubted, and by himself generously admitted, indebtedness to Rembrandt makes it appropriate for us to approach an estimate of what he himself accomplished by way of a comparison between him and Rembrandt; and we can perhaps do this without any injustice to the later artist. He was well aware of Rembrandt's greatness; it is not too much to say that his admiration had something of the enthusiasm of a devotee. How he estimated himself in comparison may be gathered from his saying, *à propos* of a portrait long attributed to Rembrandt, but of which the attribution had recently been questioned. "I am sure it is not his. I could have painted it myself; but I could not paint a Rembrandt."

We have seen what he learned from Rembrandt in his youth. In the story of the Spanish journey he gives his mature judgment of him. He is in the Prado at Madrid with his friends. A French acquaintance appeals to him to endorse an enthusiastic estimate of Velasquez; whereupon one of his fellow-travellers mentions a present-day tendency to rank the Spanish higher than the Dutch master. Israëls will have none of it. For one thing, he holds, Rembrandt is more than a painter. His etchings, even had he never used the brush, would have placed him high among the great artists. Then his great

qualities are enumerated : imagination, simplicity, the poetry of his solemn, mysterious effects, the strength and subtle skill of his craftsmanship. Velasquez never did anything like the heads in *The Syndics,* hair that is hair, eyes that do look, brows that wrinkle. He can greatly enjoy Velasquez's *Las Lanzas ;* but *The Night Watch* is a miracle, unequalled in its brushwork, imaginatively true to life, and possessing a witchery of light and shade of which Rembrandt alone possesses the secret. He combined in himself, says Israëls, the mysticism of the North, and the glow and supreme artistry of the South. Velasquez's art is calm and untroubled ; he achieves without effort ; his deep emotion implies no struggle ; he has made for himself a throne upon which he sits securely, while Rembrandt is sternly wrestling in the dark, and ever reaching out to the infinite and unknown ; and while the art of Velasquez is concerned only with what is immediately around him, Rembrandt is in sympathy with a wide range of human life, explores history, and seeks to imagine the unseen.

This is the substance of Israëls' estimate of Rembrandt, reached by way of comparison with

JOZEF ISRAËLS

Velasquez. After he had delivered it, his French friend observed that he was warm, offered him a chocolate, and then led him away to look at a Raphael!

After telling in the "Rembrandt" of the "Masterpieces in Colour" series, of his early study of Rembrandt, Israëls asks: "What do I think of the master now, after so many years?" And then he gives a keen and enthusiastic analysis of *The Night Watch*, after which he passes to *The Syndics* again, saying: "I don't know whether this picture was very much discussed by Rembrandt's contemporaries when it was finished. But to us, who have seen so much of the art of the great Italians, Germans, and Spaniards, these heads are the highest achievement of the art of painting." His enthusiasm for this picture is unbounded, for he goes on to recall that when he was in Madrid he and his companions went into an exhibition of works by modern Spanish artists, and saw there a copy of it made by a Spanish painter when on a visit to Holland. He does not know, he says, whether it was national prejudice or conviction, "but this copy spoke to us of a spirit of greater simplicity, of a truer

conception of the nature and dignity of mankind, than anything we had admired in the Prado"; and he adds that the picture kills its own Dutch brothers, makes Van der Helst look superficial, and Frans Hals unfinished and flat: "so much thoroughness combined with such freedom and grace of movement is not to be found anywhere else."

The value that these appreciations have for us is not so much that they show what Israëls was as a critic, as a discerner of what is good and great in art—though this is within the scope of this book—but that they come from one of whom we can certainly say that he was of the lineage of Rembrandt. Israëls, in expounding Rembrandt, is explaining himself. As a youth he had copied the head of one of the Syndics, and had gone from the study of Rembrandt's works to see the modern counterparts of them in actual life in the streets of Amsterdam. Becoming in later life a leader among those who turned Dutch art back again to the interpretation of Dutch life, the task it had so splendidly accomplished in the seventeenth century, it is of Rembrandt, above all the other masters of that time, that he reminds us.

JOZEF ISRAËLS

Not, however, in the technique of his portraits; there he calls to mind the bravura of Frans Hals; only he has Rembrandt's feeling for atmosphere— with a difference—and a greater intensity in his study of character than Hals possessed.

We must not expect him to have all the qualities of his great ancestor. He does not move easily, as did Rembrandt, in the realm of history. His art, his whole outlook on life, was too homely for this. Nor could he, or at least did he, marshal together a number of men, as did Rembrandt in *The Night Watch*, *The Syndics*, and the *Anatomy Lesson*, and not only group them into artistic unity, but bring them into living relation with each other, while marking clearly their diverse individual characteristics. Israëls' art also lacks the monumental, the magisterial air, we may say, of that of Rembrandt; he has not the same massive forms, the same resonant tones, his light-and-shade delights us only: that of Rembrandt thrills us, makes the pulse beat faster; at times it fills us with awe, as if out of the depth of shade some dread portent would come forth.

The two meet, one thinks, in a quality upon

44

JOZEF ISRAËLS

which Israëls seizes when he ascribes to Rembrandt pre-eminently a spirit of great simplicity and a true conception of the nature and dignity of mankind. In these things, surely, Israëls is wholly of the lineage of Rembrandt. Were they not what he was appropriating, or, we may say, were they not moulding his artistic nature, when he was working and studying at the Trippenhuis? They were latent in him perhaps—qualities inherent in his race. Rembrandt stirred them into activity and strengthened them ; and, in due time, Zandvoort did the rest.

By simplicity we understand here a single-minded devotion to one great aim that puts aside all that is irrelevant to it. It is St. Paul's "this one thing I do." Israëls was recognising the need for it when he spoke of the things he must not paint. And the aim was no mean one. It was that which he attributes to Rembrandt: to set forth "a true conception of the nature and dignity of mankind." Do we hesitate to accept the word "dignity"? Only, I think, if we use it in a narrow, inadequate sense. There is more of the dignity of trained intelligence, of place and power, of *savoir faire*, about Rembrandt's people

45

than about those of Israëls. Some of them
are almost demigods. As that confident com-
mander, Captain Banning Coq, comes striding
out of the gloom into the full light, we prepare
quickly to step aside, lest we should get in his
way and draw down his anger upon us. Rembrandt's subjects were the governing, directing
men of his day, and his women, even in old age,
mostly look capable and self-possessed, and but
rarely pathetic. Israëls was usually among the
poor in circumstances, and often among the poor
in spirit. It was the dignity of the labour that
supports the humblest cottage home, of the
mother's care for her child, of the brave facing
of danger, of patient submission to the frailty
and suffering of old age, and to the unescapable
decree of death, that Israëls saw, felt, and recorded. This is the simple but profound interpretation of some of the basic facts of human
life that he gives in his works. Even his portraits speak to us of patient thought or deeply
quiet feeling rather than of resolute directing
or governing force.

Israëls did not then become a mere understudy
of Rembrandt. He accomplished something in

JOZEF ISRAËLS

the same kind as that which Rembrandt had accomplished ; but it was complementary, not mere repetition. His art, on the technical side, differs from that of Rembrandt in accordance with the difference of its content. The two are at one in the rigorous exclusion of non-essentials ; Israëls' more intimate subjects admit of more detail than those of Rembrandt ; but the detail is almost invariably kept in its right place. The deep solemnity of Rembrandt's light-and-shade would be out of place in Israëls' cottages ; but he knows how to vary his own rendering of light-and-shade so that it becomes a symbol of changing human moods and conditions. What could more profoundly express the hour of desolation than the grey light from the distant window dying along the cheerless room in the *Alone in the World*, reproduced in this volume ? Israëls' light-and-shade lacks the intensity of that of Rembrandt, but he can make it nobly expressive ; and his delight in the interplay of light and dark is almost an obsession with him.

A massive sense of power in form and tone, again, would less well serve Israëls' ends than

the broken lines that suggest breathing and
moving life, and seem to take us within the
picture, amongst the people there, and bring
us into intimate relations with them.

The single word that serves most aptly to
describe the difference between Rembrandt and
Israëls is that the latter was the more homely of
the two, both in his art and in his interpretation.
They may be likened to two brothers, one of
whom has gone out into the world and won for
himself a place there, while the other has remained
quietly in the village home. We need not here
try to assess all that this difference means by
reckoning up the relative value of the virtues and
joys of home-life, and of those that arise out of
the wider human relations. It is enough if we
have arrived at the nature of the difference, and
also of the resemblance between the great Dutch
master of the seventeenth century and his suc-
cessor in the nineteenth, so that we may be
able the better, by comparison and contrast, to
enjoy the art of both, and in particular of the
one whose art we have set ourselves to study
here.

We must now rank ourselves with those of

48

COURTSHIP.

whom Israëls spoke as seeing the poet in the picture, with the limitation that we think we do not see the poet only and forget the art of painting. We recollect that while Israëls said that he only chose his subjects for their line and colour, he did not deny that there was poetry in them, and that he was gratified to know it to have been appreciated.

Perhaps we shall be better able fully to enjoy Israëls' treatment of subjects in which he succeeded if we first briefly take note of those in which he either failed or only achieved a moderate success. Such are his historical pictures. If, after at Zandvoort turning away from historical subjects to the life round about him, he had never attempted again to call up the past, we should have lost little that is worth the having. He chose subjects for the successful treatment of which he was singularly ill-equipped. In his genre pictures his drawing of the human figure is by no means always accurate. Also a measure of clumsiness of form and action is not out of place in representations of fisher-folk and peasantry. But something different from this is needed for biblical or other mythical subjects requiring the nude. Under the

JOZEF ISRAËLS

title *The Source*, Israëls gives, not a nymph, but a by no means beautifully-formed young woman, apparently not very strong in the back, seated by a stream-side. It is merely a nude study of a bather. His *Adam and Eve* is only two naked figures in a more or less impressionist landscape. So also with his *Temptation of Eve*. If not actually badly drawn, the figure of Eve is at best wholly lacking in beauty. She is a modern woman, not in a garden, but in uncultivated, woodland country. At first we are puzzled why she should be there in a state of absolute nudity. Then we see that a serpent is coming towards her with an apple in his mouth. This incident might be credible were the rest of the subject not treated so realistically. As it is, if we do not dismiss it at once as an absurdity, we find ourselves disposed to be no more serious than to note that the serpent must have brought the fruit from a considerable distance; for there is not an apple-tree in sight, nor is there likely to be one in such surroundings. The lack of imagination of the kind necessary for a proper treatment of such subjects is nothing short of ludicrous. These, surely, are among the things

50

A DUTCH FISHER GIRL

By kind permission of Messrs. Wallis & Son

that Israëls should have known he ought not to paint.

His *David Playing before Saul*, reproduced at p. 33, is more successful, chiefly because the subject does not depend upon mastery of the nude, and approximates to genre. At the same time, both the subject and Israëls' rendering of it rise high above the level of an everyday event. The artist has treated it in a nobly imaginative way. We are inside the royal tent facing its opening, of which the upper part is outside the picture; and this, together with the far-reaching prospect of valley, river, town, and distant mountains, with a brilliant light-filled sky above, gives great impressiveness to the scene. The king lies uneasily on his couch, his head resting on his right hand; his left arm is stretched out, and the hand is clenched. His face is in dark shade. Behind him is his spear. A female attendant—his daughter, Michal?—sits by his side, with bowed head. At the other side of the tent-opening is David, playing on his harp, while he gazes into the light which illumines his figure. The contrast is finely drawn between the innocent, fresh spirit of youth, and the troubled spirit of the

JOZEF ISRAËLS

man of years whose conscience convicts him of
evil. The Hebrew painter has been moved to a
fine pictorial utterance by one of the most tra-
gically pathetic of Hebrew stories. We cannot,
therefore, regret that Israëls did not wholly con-
fine himself to painting the humbler among the
people of his own country. But it was amongst
them that in every way his greatest work was
done. His spirit and his methods were too
homely for sustained success in the field of
myth and history. Like the dyer's hand, we say
again, they became subdued to that in which they
habitually worked.

Turning, then, to his rendering of everyday life,
we note, what has already been incidentally mentioned, that in his earlier work he was not averse
to a measure of sensationalism. He often struck
the pathetic and the tragic notes. If, as he says,
he did not stop to consider whether or not the
public would like what he painted, it was none
the less the pictures of this kind that first drew
general attention to him. *The Drowned Fisherman*, now in our National Gallery, is said to have
established his reputation outside his own country.
Did he consciously acquire a distaste for this kind

52

of appeal? Certainly he abandons it in his later pictures, and on the side of subject, as we have already had to say with regard to detail, we may as well leave his pictures alone if we will not be content with the most ordinary happenings of daily life. One might suppose him to have become more cheerful and content as the years went by; and it is surely possible for age to face life's pathos and tragedy more calmly than youth can face them, because age is better able to evaluate the ethical and spiritual gains that come through them. The buoyancy of youth and the thoughtfulness of age are combined in the account of his Spanish journey. The last paragraph in it shows how calmly he could think of one of life's greatest losses that had come to him, and quite simply and naturally take his readers into his confidence, undoubting of the sympathy even of those who were unknown to him, and to whom he was personally unknown. "To the reader who has followed me so far," he writes, "I will only say that we arrived home safe and sound. Our families and friends congratulated us on our safe return from our wanderings. But the hand which once was the most eagerly extended to

53

welcome me home, that hand was no longer there."

It is such a spirit of calm acceptance of what life brings, of its sorrows as well as of its joys, of its gains as well as of its losses, that breathes from his pictures. Did it exhale from the simple people whom he made the subject of his art; and while he was consciously thinking mainly of lines and colours, was he, in this deep sense, becoming one of them? It is commonly believed that farmers are always grumbling at the weather. One's experience is that it is difficult to get them to do so. They learn to trust, if not in Providence, at any rate in a law of averages in which the seasons have given them confidence. Many of us must have been shamed by the cheerfulness of those whose lot has seemed to us to be intolerably hard.

For such reasons as these we may well doubt the conclusion arrived at by some who have discussed Israëls' work: that he was ever insisting on the privations and the sorrows of the poor. What his pictures tell us rather is that, as to the deepest essentials of life, the poor are no worse off—oftener, perhaps, better off—in their

cottages than the millionaires in their mansions ; which, however, let me hasten to say, will only be used by a mean soul as an argument against social and economic betterment. What Israëls began to gather at Zandvoort was material for his art as a painter, and a thoroughly sane and wholesome outlook upon life. Neither with regard to himself, nor in his thoughts about others, was there anything bordering on the morbid or the pessimistic. This is what we should expect in a Jew who was also a Dutch-man. This is what those who knew him well say of him. This is what both his story of the Spanish journey and his pictures make clear to those who did not know him personally.

Herr Meier-Graeffe, to whom Israëls' colour is brown sauce, says also that with Israëls Dutch painting became sentimental for the first time. If we admit this, it is still true in a depreciatory sense only with respect to a small number of his paintings, and those chiefly early ones—the ones in which we have been obliged to see a touch at least of melodrama. Nothing could be further from the truth than to call the main body of his work sentimental, or to consider this a characteristic of the man himself. It is a mistake that could only be made by one to whom the expression by art of generous emotion, of simple, natural fellow-feeling, was something to be avoided. Israëls certainly brings us into close sympathetic relations with those to whom he introduces us; and one knows well the type of critic to whom such a quality in a picture is not merely unnecessary, but an actual offence and cause of irritation. But this quality is not sentiment in any depreciatory sense of the word. Therefore we do not regret that it is much more conspicuous in his work than in that of the earlier Dutch masters. We are interested, often keenly interested, in their people; we feel with those of Israëls. He strikes a deeper, more intimate, human note.

It is instructive to contrast him in this respect with Millet, from whom Israëls' inspiration did not immediately come any more than it immediately came from Rembrandt. Meier-Graeffe says that Israëls saw in Rembrandt and in Millet only that which may be reduced to a formula. This means that his art was little or nothing more than a compound of that of the other two painters. He was an eclectic, in this case—not an

MOTHER'S TASKS.

artist whose main sources of inspiration were life and nature. If he had. been only this he must have given up historical painting, and have begun his alleged efforts to combine Rembrandt and Millet before he went to Zandvoort. He does, in a sense, combine the two, not because he tried to do so, but because, in his paintings, he is more intimately in touch with individual life and character than either of the others. Rembrandt's people awaken in us an intellectual rather than an emotional interest. Millet's people are usually little more than types; they call forth our sympathy for a class rather than for individuals. Ruskin, on seeing reproductions of some of Millet's pictures, remarked that he did not show the face. Millet himself said, in a letter to Sensier, "The most joyful thing I know is the peace, the silence, that one enjoys in the woods or on the tilled lands. One sees a poor, heavily-laden creature with a bundle of faggots advancing from a narrow path in the fields. The manner in which this figure comes suddenly before one is a momentary reminder of the fundamental condition of human life, toil. On the tilled land around one watches figures hoeing and digging.

JOZEF ISRAËLS

One sees how this or that one rises and wipes away the sweat with the back of his hand. ' In the sweat of thy face shalt thou eat bread.' Is that merry, enlivening work, as some people would like to persuade us? And yet it is here that I find the true humanity, the great poetry." Here men and women are so many toiling creatures, no more individualised than we individualise the bees as we watch them incessantly leaving and re-entering the hive. We may say that the difference between Millet's and Israëls' people is that while the former are figures, the latter are pre-eminently faces. Millet knew those toilers individually, but he rarely shows us that he so knew them. Israëls knew his people individually, and he gives us as much of his own intimate knowledge of them as he can.

In the above quotation from Millet we cannot but recognise a morbid strain. It may be that his peasantry had, if not a harder life, still a less cheerful one than that of Israëls' people. " Is that merry, enlivening work?" asks Millet. I thought of the difference between him and Israëls one day—and it was a grey winter's day too—when, at Scheveningen, I saw a fisherman's

58

daughter having a merry romp with a dog, a group of fisher-lads boisterously enjoying a game, and a fisherman trying to catch a little lad, who nimbly dodged hither and thither and long eluded his big pursuer, to the immense delight of his playfellows, while a woman looked on with obvious enjoyment of the simple fun. The poor, "in a lump," are not miserable, any more than they are, as Tennyson's Northern Farmer declared them to be, bad.

It is only rarely that a picture by Israëls brings Millet to mind, except in the general sense that they both usually had the toiling poor for a subject. We do not say of many of Israëls' pictures "That is like a Millet," much less "Is that a Millet?" One of the pictures reproduced here, *Sheltering from the Storm*, (page 67), is an exception to this rule. It does remind us of Millet, and yet when we look carefully at it we know it for Israëls'. It is Israëls' in the treatment of the landscape, in the comfortable look of the shepherd, even in a certain sprightliness about the dog and the sheep. To regard Israëls as being a kind of interpreter of Millet to Holland is not in accordance with the facts. Though Millet was ten years older than Israëls, he had only just left the studio of Delaroche when the latter entered it. The year in which, after trying to make a living by painting pictures after the style of Boucher and Fragonard, Millet painted the first of his great peasant pictures, *The Winnower*, was the year that Israëls left Paris, soon to come to his awakening at Zandvoort. In 1857 Israëls exhibited at the Paris Salon two seashore pictures. In 1859 Millet's *Death and the Woodcutter* was rejected at the Salon. If we call Israëls the Dutch Millet, it must be by way of comparison, not of affiliation; and we must be at liberty to call Millet the French Israëls.

What, then, we get from Israëls, comparing him with Rembrandt and Millet, is a no less individual, but more friendly, intimate knowledge of his people than the former gives us, and a much more individual knowledge and a more cheery idea of them than Millet gives. There is a tonic power in Israëls' pictures, just as there is in the mere neighbourhood of the fisherman or the peasant, the builder or

the weaver, of those who are doing the fundamental work of life, and by whose labour alone,
and by the counsel and inventiveness they could
supply, there could be a true, if simple, civilisa-
tion ; whereas, so much that some of us think
we could not do without is preclusive of it.
The poor may well seek to free themselves
from grinding poverty and degrading labour ;
at the same time they may rejoice that they are
spared the trouble about many things that so
often belittles the life of the rich, unable to
sound the deeps of life because they are ever
demanding some shallow, new thing.   Love,
and the hopes and fears, the joys and sorrows,
that love brings, are not less open—are perhaps
more open—to the poor than to the rich ; and
they can dream dreams for themselves and for
their children, alongside which one shudders
to think of the dreams of avarice.   It is such
essential life that Israëls' pictures set before us.
His people are earnestly, nobly, spiritually living.
They toil, but not without—nay, therefore all the
more with—faith, and hope, and love.   In saying
this, is one guilty of reading something into the
pictures?   No one who had seen the portrait of

JOZEF ISRAËLS

a working woman, entitled *Faith's Trustfulness*, would make this accusation.

Israëls does not often let us see his people at play. I can recall no picture in which "grownups" are playing, with the exception of cardplaying, which we take for granted among nearly all sorts and conditions of people. They are either working or resting from work—until the final rest. Some of the happiest people many of us have known, rarely, if ever, probably, played a game throughout their lives, which is not to say that games are not good, but only that they are not wholly indispensable—at least to those who work in the open air, who fish the sea, or plough the land. The only open-air play that Israëls shows us, even among the children, is the sailing of toy boats in the shallow water on the shore, and this, in the case of fishermen's children, becomes almost symbolical. It is play, yet more than play. We think of Wordsworth's

> " And see the children sport upon the shore,
> And hear the mighty waters rolling evermore."

This almost uniform occupation of his people with the work that life and love demand, or at

ZANDVOORT FISHERWOMEN

By kind permission of Messrs. Bousson, Valadon & C.

JOZEF ISRAËLS

most their enjoyment of intervals of rest, gives to
his pictures an epic quality. These simple folk
are of the kind that belongs to all time. Fashion
and invention distinguish them in no essential
particular from their predecessors of centuries
ago. They are much like the people whom we
meet where history begins. If we go to see them
in real life, and find the products of modern in-
dustry in their shops and houses, we receive a
shock at the intrusion of such irrelevant triviali-
ties. We find none of them in Israëls' pictures.
Is it superstition or what, that, being a townsman
who has lived many years in the country, I never
feel really at ease in the company of a peasant,
always suspecting that he thinks very little of me
and my doings, even though he be outwardly
deferential? Religious and political systems come
and go, but such people as these, and the work
they do, remain. Epic poems, the dictionaries
tell us, relate the achievements of heroes. Well,
" peace hath her victories no less renowned than
war," and such people as Israëls' toilers are the
world's indispensable heroes—the world could
well have spared many, if not most, of those
whose praises have been most loudly sung—so

JOZEF ISRAËLS

we repeat that the pictures in which they are made real to us have an epic quality, even if they be not epic, or historical, in form.

Was this the painter's intention? We might content ourselves with saying that this epic quality is in the people themselves and their surroundings, and that the artist has insensibly incorporated it in his work. Not every artist, however, who has made the peasantry the subject of his pictures has expressed it; and we might well assume a feeling for it, sub-conscious or dimly conscious it might be, to be an element in Israëls' mental and ethical temperament. But I think there is evidence that this was so. We find it in that invaluable story of the Spanish journey. It shows itself in what has already been quoted here from the story. Let us take another instance. He is in the crowded, noisy market at Tangier. An Arab comes along with a string of camels; he has just arrived from Fez, after a fortnight's journey across the desert, and is looking for a place to unload his beasts; both he and they are covered with grey dust. Israëls and his companions at once think of the patriarchal stories, and could take this man to be Eliezer on his way

64

ON THE LOOK OUT

JOZEF ISRAËLS

to find a wife for Isaac. Any one familiar with
the Bible, it may be said, would have made some
such comparison. Precisely : because familiarity
with the Bible does induce a large imaginative
view of human life in all but the shallow-minded ;
and one would be surprised to find that Israëls, a
Jew, was without it.

We have direct evidence of it also in his pictures.
It is clear in the one of the old Jewish scribe
at Tangier ; and, again, in the one reproduced
at page 28, *A Son of the Old Folk*. A less
imaginative artist might have given the picture
the title *A Jewish Pawnbroker*. But no. This
man who sits on his doorstep, surrounded by what
may be called waifs and strays and outcasts of the
things that people commonly use, is a link in the
chain that stretches back to the patriarchs. Is he
thinking of profits and losses as he sits there
with bent head, and seemingly oblivious of
everything about him ? Surely he would not
have looked so dreamy had such things been in
his mind. The title suggests a contrast between
his condition and surroundings and his lineage.
Has not his race dreams of a great future
which the humblest member of it may share ?

JOZEF ISRAËLS

Thus may many a Hebrew have sat dreaming beside the waters of Babylon. The picture is an epic of exile. Israëls painted several versions of this subject, all of them different in details, the one reproduced here in the important particular that there is a child between the old man's knees —another link in the chain.

The manner of Israëls' later painting contributes largely to the epic quality of his works by its subordination of all detail, and its insistence on simply house, field, sea, sun, and air. " Do not ask him," says his friend Jan Veth, " to give you harmonious grace or sustained rapture. He would drag you through the involved picturesqueness of squalid existences. Is this part of his Jewish descent, and is it the fact that an Israelite is by nature unable to take an objective view of the visible world for the mere pleasure of the eye, that an object does not arouse his true sympathy till he can see in it an embodiment of some human thought and feeling?" Similarly Stahl, writing of him as a Jewish artist, says : " As do the words used by a true poet, so do the things that Israëls paints recover their aboriginal significance. They exert their full strength on our innermost soul, with-

SHELTERING FROM THE STORM

By kind permission of Messrs. Wallis & Son

out being driven home with help of many adjectives." Again the same writer says : "Israëls is not a realist; he gives, not a piece of the visible world, but the spirit that informs it. He is not an epic artist, who sets forth only the thing itself, but a lyrical artist, who distils the essence of its being"; which, perhaps, does not contradict what I have said about an epic quality in his work. Similarly Mr. Konody says : "If ever there was a painter whose work betrays contempt of material, or at least oblivion of material, in his complete absorption in the psychology and true inwardness of his subjects, it surely is Jozef Israëls."

It might have been expected beforehand that one who united in himself the home-loving character of the Dutch people and the positive tendency of the Jewish religion would fully realise and express the poetry of simple family life ; that he would see in it no small part of essential religion ; and this is what Israëls did. We need not disparage those who, like Dante and Blake, weave for us worlds of the imagination, in order to realise our indebtedness to those who show us that the place whereon we stand is holy ground. Still, to pierce through the heart of the known

and visible may be a greater thing than to give
form to the unseen. Indeed, is not the form so
given only a reflection of what we know and
see, and not unseldom a distorted and misleading
one? Israëls, the painter of humble household
scenes, was more truly a seer and a prophet, a
sounder interpreter of the essential things of life,
than many upon whom these titles have been
formally bestowed.

Turning now from these general considerations
to the pictures themselves, we note that, though
landscape plays an important part in Israëls'
work, he did not paint purely landscape pictures.
It was exclusively used as a setting for figures.
All the same, it is worth attention on its own
account ; and not a few of his pictures would be
fine landscapes if the figures were absent. With
the limitation imposed by the main purpose of his
work, we clearly cannot expect from him a search
for the exceptionally beautiful in nature, or a de-
tailed rendering of her intricate beauties of form
and colour. I had written first " the exceptionally
beautiful or sublime in nature," but I struck out
" or sublime," for surely nothing is more sublime
than the quite ordinary things that appear in

JOZEF ISRAËLS

Israëls' pictures. There are the great immensities of sky and ocean. There are the sunlight and the atmosphere—the breathing sphere—there is the fruitful earth. We are unhealthy in mind and spirit if these things are not always sublime to us, even under the most ordinary conditions.

Israëls' sky is a great space through which light comes to us. In the evening the light fails, and gathers itself in on the horizon, while clouds that hardly temper the heat of the mid-day sun now look dark in the upper sky; because the night cometh when no man can work. We have a fine example of the light-filled space in *Courtship* (p. 48), and of the evening sky in *The Way Across the Fields* (p. 76). In another picture a woman is crossing the open country in the evening, carrying a child. The crescent moon is shining, and its light gently suffuses everything. In the west the light is almost gone out of the last red glow, leaving it little more than dead colour. There is the same deadness, a mere smoulder, in the sky in Millet's *Angélus*. In another picture two women stand by a farmhouse in the moonlight. Everything breathes tranquillity. As we look at the picture we are

69

JOZEF ISRAËLS

grateful to Wordsworth for his simple phrase, "the moonlight air." It is not merely the sight but the feeling of light that we get. In *Courtship* we feel the light above and about us; it dazzles and it warms.

Of the sea Israëls makes no varied studies. We can say if we like that he had a formula for it. The formula, if we so put it, is water moving in waves. Again we feel as well as see. I need not refer specifically to illustration after illustration in this book in which the water looks, to put it quite simply, like a liquid that would wet us and in which we should sink. The avoidance of all hard lines, and hints of reflections here and there, give it this appearance. It is made sufficiently rough in many of the pictures to suggest danger. This is all that the artist needs. The fisher-folk, it reminds us, follow a calling that often brings them face to face with death.

Of the land that borders the ocean Israëls shows us little more than the sand-dunes, with the long, gray-green grasses bent by the wind, and, farther inland, the fields, with growth of grass or of corn. At times the prospect is soon closed in because the ground rises, at others it

stretches away—a few horizontal brush-strokes giving the suggestion—into the far distance.

These landscapes of Israëls, so simple in content, so rich in the emotion they awaken, constantly recall some of Tennyson's landscape descriptions, or, rather, impressions, such as the "Yet oft when sundown skirts the moor" of *In Memoriam*, "The level waste, the rounding grey" of *Mariana;* and, in the same poem,

> " But when the moon was very low,
>   And wild winds bound within their cell,
>   The shadow of the poplar fell
>   Upon her bed, across her brow."

The landscapes on the arras in *The Palace of Art* also convey strong, clear impressions "without being driven home by aid of many adjectives," to quote again Stahl's observation of this quality in Israëls' art :—

> " One seem'd all dark and red—a tract of sand,
>   And some one pacing there alone,
>   Who paced for ever in a glimmering land
>   Lit with a low large moon.

> " One show'd an iron coast and angry waves.
>   You seem'd to hear them climb and fall
>   And roar rock-thwarted under bellowing caves,
>   Beneath the windy wall."

JOZEF ISRAËLS

Here are the most ordinary things. Yet what
do they become when the poet interprets them?
So it is with Israëls' renderings of the Dutch
coast and fields : for he, also, was a poet.

Israëls was not blind to the softer and more
luxuriant side of nature's beauty. It was not
because he could not see it, and it made no appeal
to him, that he did not paint it. Driving out
from Seville, under a blazing sun that withered
up everything, he turned with longing to Holland,
to the drive along the Amstel to the *Kalfje*, or
from The Hague to Delft by way of Rijswijk,
amid trees, fields, and water. But these were
evidently among the things that he felt he ought
not to paint. He left them to others. He was
not alone. We shall say more of this shortly.
What he left untouched was done, better than he,
with other things urgent upon him, could have
done it, by Jacob and Willem Maris, by Anton
Mauve, and others.

But the landscape in his pictures is never more
than a setting for figures, which are his main
subject. It has already been said that he puts
us on intimate terms with his people, and it is
time for us to become acquainted with them.

LITTLE JANE

JOZEF ISRAËLS

Staying in a carpenter's house at Zandvoort, he would inevitably get an intimate knowledge of the life of the little fishing village. Afterwards he had a corner of an old Dutch cottage built up in the studio of his house at The Hague, while he used a glass house when painting open-air subjects—sketches, studies, and memory being then sufficient for him.

The cottages in which his people live are lighted by small and small-paned windows, near to which the women and girls sit to do their spinning or sewing. The light is good there, but it dies away at the sides and towards the back of the room. The floors are brick, or stone, or bare boards. There is the Dutch tiled fireplace; there is a wooden bed, a box with one side out, against the wall. The furniture is of the simplest—strong wooden chairs and table. Simple also are the household utensils; the frying-pan is much in evidence. There are metal and earthenware jugs that would delight the collector; but they are familiar everyday things to the cottagers. An old clock, with uncased weights, hangs on the wall above the table by which the widow sits disconsolate; we can almost hear its measured ticking in the melancholy silence. These details do not obtrude themselves; we see them if we look curiously about the room. Otherwise we merely know that the things are there; that we are in a house provided with what its occupants require. There is neither too much nor too little; our attention is not withdrawn from the people by either crowded detail or a bareness that suggests distressful poverty. In the Haarlem picture, *Refreshment*, reproduced at page 80, there is far more detail than usual. It is not as much in evidence in the reproduction as in the original picture, where it fussily distracts attention. This is an exception, for, as Stahl puts it, Israëls does not analyse, he composes.

Going with Israëls into these houses we find, not much to our surprise, that the men are generally out. We find one man at home, but he is ill in bed, and two neighbours have come in to visit him. Israëls was a witness of this incident, stored it up in his mind, and painted it many years afterwards. In another house two men are seated, talking, while a woman cooks something for them in the frying-pan. *A Dutch Interior* shows the husband enjoying a pipe,

JOZEF ISRAËLS

none the less because wife and children are with him ; while in *A Frugal Meal* (p. 20), we have the family dinner-party, with the baby in the cradle brought close up so that the mother may look after it while she superintends the meal. Generally, however, the women are alone. Of course, the men are out fishing, or working in the fields. But if we go out we shall not see them ; at least we shall see more women than men. Israëls rarely shows us any but household work going on. There is a photograph of himself and his son out in a sailing-boat, but he does not show us the fishermen at work out at sea ; we must be content to see them riding on horseback through the surf from their boats, or carrying in the anchor, or a man, again on horseback, at the edge of the surf, waving a flag as a signal of danger to an incoming boat. Once we catch sight of a man with a long-handled net getting shellfish or shell, the latter to be used as gravel for one thing, in the shallow water. Nor shall we find the sower or the reaper in the field, but only a field-worker resting on his long-handled spade, or a party of field-workers returning home, or an old man walking along the edge of a corn-

75

JOZEF ISRAËLS

field, carrying a rake or a scythe, and holding
by the hand a little girl—grandfather and grand-
child, who are devoted to each other, is what it
looks like.   What examples there are of Israëls'
showing men hard at work by or on the sea or
in the field, are only exceptions to the rule that
he suggests such work, but does not show it.

He suggests it often by the relation of the
women and the children to it.   One is reminded
of Charles Kingsley's " Three Fishers "; not that
Israëls harps upon that melancholy string, but
that in his pictures, as in the poem, the women
and the children are not only not forgotten, but
are given their due prominence.   Israëls does
not ask us to think always of the women as
weeping while the men work.   Even a picture
of a woman, seated high on the sand-dune, may
be merely *Dolce far Niente;* but another is *The
Wide Wide Sea*, and in another, *On the Look
Out*, there is anxiety written on the face of the
mother, who, with a child in her lap, is intently
watching for a distant sail.   We think of Gaud,
in Pierre Loti's " Pêcheur d'Islande," when all
the boats but her husband Yann's have returned
to harbour, stealing away to the lonely cross on

76

THE WAY ACROSS THE FIELDS.

the cliff from which the wide expanse of ocean can be seen, and watching there day after day and throughout the day. That such things may be is the price that has to be paid for the full joy of a safe return home. That Israëls deeply felt this, not only *The Drowned Fisherman* shows, but his inability to pass without stopping to look at the woman whom he saw at Algeciras.

There is suggestion of the husband being at sea, while the wife works at home, in a sick-bed picture—the bed a veritable cupboard with mounting-steps to it ; the woman who is taking care of the invalid is mending a net. Then we see the women and children crossing the dunes, with baskets on their backs, as in the picture reproduced at p. 62 ; and what thorough working-women they look, bronzed and muscular, and with feet and hands that by no means conform to conventional standards in point of size. Else-where a girl with a basket on her back is wading through shallow water ; and again, p. 96, we have the happy expectancy of the child who has seated herself on the sand, and set down her basket, and looks out to sea.

In the house, where, as already said, we rarely

find the men, there is usually either a woman alone, or a woman with one or two children, and the incident is one of the simplest, particularly in the later pictures. It is in the earlier ones that we are shown a frugal meal and grace before meat. It is in an earlier one also that we see a sick woman, leaning back against a pillow in her arm-chair, and hardly able to smile as she watches her little child with difficulty carrying a stool on which to sit beside her, while cupboard, ladder, clothes-basket, lantern, and other things are carefully depicted, and there are patches, not a diffusion, of light and shade.

Though we have refused, and still refuse, to think of Israëls as caring only for line and colour, or, as we think, light, atmosphere, and tone, we are constrained to think that the keen interest he had in them—bewitchment was what he felt it to be—influenced his choice of subject, and was in part, at least, the reason why he repeated the same subject again and again with little more change than a variation of the light and colour. He could satisfy his deep artistic need without representing vigorous action; nay, indeed, vigorous action might compete too much with the

MAKING PANCAKES

JOZEF ISRAËLS

interest of light playing upon and around the figure and dying away in the recesses of the room. Be this as it may—and it is not possible to dogmatise about it—there is no stir and bustle in these household scenes. None the less they are intensely real; what we see is what does happen, and has deep, if simple, human significance.

How wholly delightful, how truly sympathetic in the rendering, is *Mother's Tasks* (page 56). The pleasure taken by the artist in the play of light is obvious in the reproduction. But in the treatment of the subject, note how the mother has to stretch round the child asleep on her knee in order to do her sewing; and how true is the incident of the older child, who is not too old to be afraid of the hen that is pecking up what of eatable has fallen on the floor. The absent worker is suggested by the spade in the corner. Through the window we can see other cottages, and a church spire, which not only suggests that high things enter into and ennoble the life of this toiling mother, but, small though it be, is by no means without its value in the composition.

Another delightful picture of mother and child

is the one reproduced at page 59. It is of no
use for Israëls to tell us, when he has painted
such a child as this, with its toes cocked up, and
literally fisting the food into its mouth, that he
was concerned only with purely artistic considerations, and did not stop to consider whether or not
the public would care for what he painted. He
must have wanted this youngster to be appreciated. It deserves appreciation more even than
the beautiful, vibrating light. So does the mother,
entirely in earnest about the care of her child,
stirring the food with the spoon so that it shall
not be too hot for the little one. Both this and
the last-mentioned picture well exemplify what
has been said about the naturalness of Israëls'
treatment of his subjects. How comes it, we
ask, that we are in the same room with these
mothers, and that they are so completely uncon-
cerned? They cannot be aware of our presence.

It is interesting to note that the action of the
child, cramming the food into his mouth, is exactly
paralleled in a Madonna and Child by Masaccio,
belonging to the Rev. A. F. Sutton, and shown
at a recent Old Masters Exhibition at the Grafton
Gallery. The Virgin is feeding the Child with

REFRESHMENT

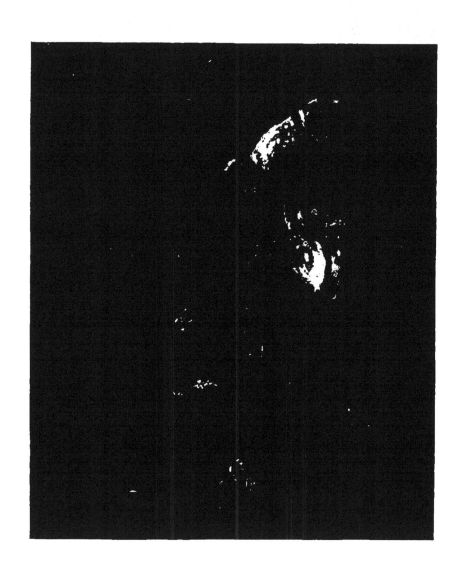

THE NEIGHBOURS

JOZEF ISRAËLS

grapes; and though this is a well-recognised symbol of the Passion, the eating is by no means symbolical, for the child is cramming them in to the utmost capacity of his mouth to hold them, and even in the sacred presence we can hardly forbear from crying out " He will choke!" Ruskin said of Giotto's Holy Family pictures that, because of their naturalism, they were essentially " Papa, Mamma, and the Baby." Well, there could have been no Holy Family pictures had not motherhood been indisputably, in itself, apart from all religious sanction, a wonderful and holy thing. Masaccio was at a point of change in art, when ordinary daily life was about to be studied frankly, for its own sake, on its own merits, and not as the ecclesiastics would have men see it. That change was first fully worked out, as we have already observed, in Holland, in the seventeenth century; and here is a Dutch painter of the nineteenth century taking us—on tiptoe, one is inclined to say— into cottage homes where mothers are tending their little ones; and we can only express the influence that the sight of them has upon us, with no halo, but the common yet so beautiful light of day about them, by saying that it is a sacrament. This, indeed, is the quality of all these pictures of Israëls; they are as radiant in the simple strength and purity of the life of the toiler, as they are beautiful in their quality of sunlight.

Do we weary of the constantly repeated placing of these cottagers at or near their windows, so that the painter may enjoy the bewitchment of light? Perhaps he has helped some of us to enjoy it only less intently than he did, and so the small-paned windows and rough walls become like home to us. Here, at the window again, a woman is seated. She has drawn aside the little curtain and is looking out; one arm rests on the window-sill, its hand under her chin, the other hand—they are big, working hands—rests on her knee. *Waiting* is the title of the picture. We may assume her to have finished her work, and to be watching for the return of her husband. She has a strong, resolute face, suggesting also a considerable sense of humour. Soon, we feel, the expectant look will suddenly quicken into a smile, and she will be up and away to the door, after pulling back to its place the

82

AT THE SPINNING WHEEL

JOZEF ISRAËLS

corner of the curtain. Her character is so clearly marked that we think that she must be an acquaintance; we know her, because the painter tells us so much about her. Why does he not come, the husband of this capable, forceful, yet kindly woman? He will come, we know; she is so certain of it. She will see him; but we shall not. We shall have had to go away before he comes. It is disappointing, for the artist has given us a vivid interest in her.

We need not be acquainted with more than a few of Israëls' pictures to know what he accomplished as an artist in rendering the appearance of people and landscape and cottage interiors under the conditions of light that "bewitched" him. But we need to know a larger number of them if we are to enjoy to the full what may be called his poem of humble Dutch life. The children play with their toy boats. Older ones watch them; carry the little ones on their back through the shallow water, or take their share of work with the fish baskets. Out on the sand-dunes, in the brilliant sunshine, we see youth and maiden who have reached the stage of courtship. In another picture, *Springtime*, a youth and

JOZEF ISRAËLS

maiden—is it the same pair?—are walking across
a field. They are not talking. They do not look
as if they had spoken a word for long enough.
He simply looks stolidly ahead. We suspect her
of a humorous feeling. There is a slight twinkle
in the eyes. Is she wondering how long it will
be before her devoted but embarrassed swain will
muster courage to speak to her? We go back to
the cottage window again, and, in *Voor den Uitzet*
("For the Trousseau"), we see—is it the same
maiden?—busily plying her needle. The annals
thus related are simple enough, as we follow them
from childhood through youth to the duties and
cares of middle life : simple, but in their simplicity
lies their irresistible appeal to us; and we are
grateful to the interpreter who has brought us
so near to—nay, made us the intimates of—these
people who will not figure individually in history,
yet without whom history would not be.

It is when we come to his pictures of old age
that we might suspect Israëls of taking a gloomy
view of life. Generally, his pictures of youth and
middle life are cheerful enough. Death, of course,
comes even then; and it is not an old woman
who, in one picture, sits by a fireless hearth, while,

84

JOZEF ISRAËLS

by dim candle-light, we can see, across the room, a coffin resting on chairs. *Alone in the World* is the title of the picture; and both the picture and the title express the first sense of utter loneliness that death brings, before the sympathy and help of friends can come in, and, slowly healing the sorely wounded heart, help to bring back again the willingness to live.

Old age asks less than this. It asks only for courage while waiting for death. In Israëls' pictures the last years of life do seem to be years of labour and sorrow. In several pictures we see old women trudging across the fields. In *Recollections* an aged woman, seated by a little window which only dimly lights her room, has put aside her spinning-wheel, and is gazing into the fire that burns on the stone floor. What is it that she calls up out of the past? Such scenes, surely, of childhood, youth, and middle age as we have seen in other pictures :

> " O memories !
> O past that is ! "

There were two left together in George Eliot's poem. Here there seems to be only one. In

JOZEF ISRAËLS

When one Grows Old an aged woman, her back
bent more with years than with her present stoop-
ing, leans over the fire with hands stretched out
to get some warmth into the thin blood that flows
so feebly through their veins. Old people are
not entirely alone. It would not do thus to interpret Israëls' pictures. But no kindness of friends,
not even the presence of children and grandchildren, can make old age other than a waiting
for death, and a loneliness in the sense that so
much that belonged to life when the pulse beat
strongly and work was a joy belongs to it now
no more. I once wished an old man, past
eighty years, who had children and grandchildren
and many friends, happy returns of his birthday.
" Do you really mean it?" he asked; and then
added, " I am a lonely old man."

Perhaps the saddest-looking of all these pictures
is the one reproduced at page 89, and bearing the
title, like another already mentioned, *Alone in the
World.* The long, bare window has a cheerless
appearance, and its distance seems to remove far
away the outside world, whose light falls directly
only on a small floor-space close to the window,
and is dim where it reaches the old woman weep-

86

JOZEF ISRAËLS

ing by the side of the bed where lies one who is either dead or dying. . The sparse furnishing of the room, and the cold, blue-grey light, add to the feeling of melancholy. But, on a stool, by the side of the weeping woman's chair, there is an open Bible. It makes a patch of light that is valuable in the composition ;· but perhaps we are not wrong in assuming that it was not for this reason alone that Israëls put it there. Some other thing would have served this purpose equally well.

Probably to others, as well as to myself, these scenes portraying the closing hours of life recall similar ones in their own country. To me they recall an English thatched cottage, with windows small as those that Israëls shows us, and a bedroom wholly in the roof, the timbers of which start from the level of the floor. In this cottage an old woman, past ninety years, lives alone ; she fears that any one who should come to look after her would be a trouble to her. Neighbours do for her what she cannot do for herself. She has a Bible, with large print, in which she reads, or others read to her. She alternates between cheerfulness and melancholy, even between confidence and despair; for her religion is such as to make possible these extremes. Her bodily strength outlasts her brain; she can no longer be left alone. Her granddaughter, who comes to take care of her, has often to call in some one to help to calm her troubled spirit. At last she has to be removed where she can have constant and trained attention. She lives but a few weeks longer. And now the cottage, which had known the changes of at least three hundred years, has been condemned, pulled down, and is being replaced by another that will be lucky if it lasts half the years of the old one. Often, when I have sat with the old woman and listened to her stories of seventy and eighty years ago, and the light from the window behind her has thrown her face into shade, while gleaming on the edge of her cap and white hair, and from the shawl over her shoulders, it has seemed to me as if I had found my way into an Israëls picture.

The poet called the children to come to him, because, when he heard them at play, the problems that perplexed him and clouded his brow utterly vanished. Old age forgets its weariness and brightens when it sees a little child. It were ill

ALONE IN THE WORLD.

to make old age and death the measure of the worth of life. Let us end our study of Israëls' humble friends with the children ; and Israëls' children are wholly delightful. There are too many of them for us to be able to think of him as having a melancholy outlook on life : and they make his poor toilers rich.

One picture is wholly given up to a baby and a kitten—besides being, of course, a study in light and shade. It is a cottage interior ; the fireplace emerges from the shade behind the child, which is seated in a wonderful baby-chair, like a pulpit with an ornamental back, rising up at last into a kind of carved finial. The structure is on wheels. Over the pulpit front the child hangs what looks like a bib with strings, and the kitten is trying to reach it. I have already mentioned a little toddler with difficulty carrying a stool so that it may sit by its sick mother. *Her Darling* is the title of the picture. Israëls often shows the little ones watching cooking operations, as in *Making Pancakes* (p. 78). How true to life is the little boy in *After the Storm*. The two women are anxious ; he is left alone at the table, while they stay by the open door. He is too young fully to understand and

JOZEF ISRAËLS

share their trouble, but he knows all is not well,
and so he is saddened. He plays with his food,
or, at best, eats it slowly and with little relish for
it. There is the same uncomprehending, childish
fear and distress in the two children clinging to
the woman who leads the sad procession in *The
Drowned Fisherman.* We may refer again to the
anxious sympathy with which the brave, bright
little lad looks up at his father in *The Way through
the Churchyard.* Clearly it is the little ones
that give the man who has lost his helpmate the
will and the courage to live. One likes, although
only the back of him is to be seen, the boy in *The
Return,* trudging along, and with the aid of his
stick, evidently doing not a little to help the tired
old woman along the road. And surely the little
girl in *On the Shore* is something more than an
excuse, or an occasion, for effects of light and
troubled sea! And so is that other one (p. 72)
going dreamily along the path through the corn-
field, delightful for her own sake as well as for
the play of vibrating light upon her and on everything around her. We take leave of the children
as they play with their toy boats in the shallow
water left by the retreating tide. We have said

90

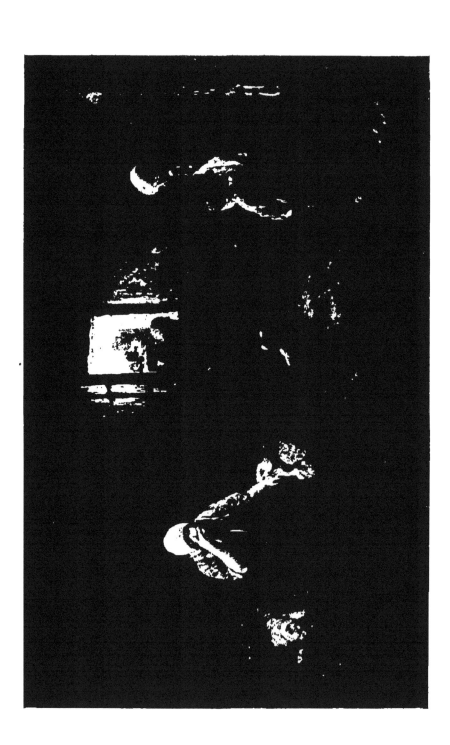

JOZEF ISRAËLS

that here they are symbolic. But when are the children not symbolic.?

Except in his portraits, Israëls rarely left his poor people. In one picture reproduced here, *The Sexton of Katwijk* (p. 97), he takes us into a class that is obviously superior, at least so far as money and what money can buy are concerned, and also, it seems, with regard to things intellectual, and to a sense of importance in the world : of counting for more than the generality of one's fellows. We have a larger window to our room, with a division down the middle of it, and a wooden frame to it. Our table is a more elegant one, to suit a gentler use ; our chairs have the same quality, and are in good condition ; we have pictures on our walls. One of us at least can write, and evidently finds no difficulty in the art, for he can smoke at the same time, using a clay pipe, the stem of which is long enough for the bowl to rest upon the table while the smoking is actually in progress. The wife quietly pursues her knitting, while she looks up, half in awe and half in admiration, at her husband who can do such wonderful things, and of whom, as to his creature wants, we may be sure she takes the greatest care. This picture is a fine piece of character-study, in addition to being an excellent example of Israëls' art.

That one has not seen or seen mention of a fisherman's or a peasant's wedding painted by Israëls is not proof that he never painted one. Courtship we know he did not overlook. A wedding of two people belonging to a more comfortable class he did paint. The picture, *A Jewish Wedding*, is in the Rijks Museum. What seems to have attracted Israëls is a particular part of the ceremony when both bride and bridegroom stand under one shawl. According to the Jewish custom, the men wear their hats, and the bridegroom's silk hat is clearly not going to be improved by having the shawl over it. He looks down affectionately at the bride as he places the ring on her finger, she watching the act with a shy, half-frightened expression. The bystanders, except those who are hidden behind more important persons, watch the proceedings intently. The picture is an interesting human document. One suspects Israëls of finding the incident of the shawl rather amusing. He has dashed the picture off hastily, the painting being unusually

CHILDREN OF THE SEA

Swasso Museum, Amsterdam

summary even for him. The picture has un-usually little value as a work of art. The figures make a series of lines, all of them approximating, at least, to the perpendicular—the shawl being responsible for several of them—and the joined hands of the bride and bridegroom, and two very obvious expedients in the accessories, fail to bring the parts of the picture into a whole. For once Israëls was attracted by a subject which he could not make pictorial, or, at least, he did not wrestle with its difficulties with sufficient earnestness to command success.

This is a convenient place to mention that, besides *The Drowned Fisherman*, our National Gallery has a small picture by Israëls, *The Philosopher*, where, once again, we are away from the physical toilers. It is, however, little more than a study of light and shade, a Rembrandtesque picture of a man writing at a table by candle-light, which dimly illumines the pictures on the wall facing him, and quickly begins to die away into gloom at each side of him.

Another picture, which finds Israels in a frankly idyllic mood, should be mentioned. It is in the Mesdag Museum at The Hague. A girl-harpist

JOZEF ISRAËLS

is seated under the trees ; the strings of her harp
come against the blue sky. The picture is a
harmony of grey and blue, relieved by warm
flesh-tones which are echoed in the lower sky.
It is visible music, and the feeling of music is
visible in the girl's expression as she plays.

It remains to say a few words about those who
were Israëls' companions in the revival of what
we may call a home-loving Dutch art, not in the
way of criticism, for that would only be appropriate
in a book dealing with modern Dutch painting as
a whole, but merely of statement, so that we may
make more clear the position of Israëls as a leader
among a number of artists who have done the
same thing in kind for their country to-day as the
great race of Dutch painters in the seventeenth
century did for it then.

The names that first come to mind are those of
Mesdag, Mauve, and Maris. Israëls, we have
seen, only painted landscape as a setting for
figures. He therefore left a large field of art
free to others. H. W. Mesdag has painted many
virile pictures of the sea and seashore, in which
often the work of the fishermen and the bluff-
bowed, broad-bottomed boats take their place.

JOZEF ISRAËLS

The pictures of his that one has seen in Dutch galleries and elsewhere leave a general impression of strong wind, driving cloud, and breakers tumbling tumultuously on the shore. Anton Mauve painted on the coast also—" big, broad coast scene ; boat just drawn up by horses," is a brief note I find of one of his pictures. Inland, anything sufficed him, for the poetry of light is everywhere. Of the three Maris brothers, Jacob and Willem were content with Dutch landscape, in town and country, painting it with all the modern feeling for light and atmosphere. The third brother, Matthew, betook himself to the world of phantasy and legend, where he saw and reported exquisitely charming people, particularly young ones. J. H. Weissenbruch paints spacious, atmospheric landscape ; and P. J. C. Gabriel is at home among the polders, the lands redeemed from the sea, where, again, light and spaciousness are the things that count. From Gerk Henkes we get both landscapes and interiors. Albert Neuhuijs takes such subjects as Israëls painted, but treats them without Israëls' depth and in brighter colour, whereby they are more likely to give pleasure to some who have a natural

95

right, we may say, to the kind of art they can enjoy. Among the portrait painters we may mention Israëls' friend, Jan Veth, and Haverman. Roelofs, already incidentally named as a portrait painter, has also painted landscapes.

Turning over note-books, I find the names of other painters and notes of pictures by them ; but all that is necessary here is to say sufficient to enable us to picture Israëls, with many other artists around him, faithfully and sympathetically interpreting life and nature. In the Dutch galleries we see, sometimes side by side, at the farthest from each other in adjoining or neighbouring rooms, pictures by Israëls and his contemporaries, including the younger generation of them ; and seeing them thus, close together, we can measure the change that began to take place in Dutch art when Israëls passed first from historical to genre painting, and then, as he worked from life and nature, broadened his style the more faithfully to interpret them.

Two other painters should at least be mentioned. J. B. Jongkind, Israëls' senior by five years, belonged to France in almost everything but birth. We link him with Boudin, in

JOZEF ISRAËLS

immediate succession to Corot, and leading up, by subtle rendering of space and atmosphere, to the Impressionists. The other painter to be named is Vincent van Gogh, born in 1853, and dying in 1890. His work, along with that of others of the so-called Post-Impressionists, who have sought significance of statement rather than mere objective truth of form or colour or atmosphere, has recently come in for both strong advocacy and vehement adverse criticism. These two painters are mentioned to show how thoroughly alive, and active in many directions, Dutch art has been during Israëls' time.

Israëls exercised over the art of his own country a profound influence, which, happily, has extended to other countries as well. Sometimes it takes the form of frank imitation, and we see pictures to which, if we caught sight of them in a Dutch gallery, we should go up expecting them to be by him. At other times it is the spirit that is in evidence, not the letter. Life and nature have been approached by the artist in his own way, but with the freshness of vision and the sympathetic interpretation with which Israëls approached them. This is the kind of influence

N   97

that Israëls had over the German artist Max
Liebermann, who found his way to him after
earlier studies at Barbizon. It was not possible
that art with so strong a vein of originality in it,
so thoughtful in the adoption of means to the end
required, so skilful in accomplishment, and giving
an interpretation so individual of life and nature,
should not arouse widespread enthusiasm and
emulation.

When Israëls died in the autumn of 1911,
those who had known him intimately mourned
the man no less then the artist. In his poem
Soothsay, Dante Rossetti deplores the state of
the man whose work is greater than himself, and
so is his own condemnation. The art of Israëls
was great—none greater in his own time, as many
think—and certainly gives him a place among
those whose name and work will long endure.
His art was the medium through which a man
of strong and simple character gave expression
to his delight in the sun-illumined world, and to
his fellow-feeling for those, and, above all, for
the humblest of those, who lived with him in it
between birth and death. The man was greater
than his work.

İNDEX

(Titles of pictures are given in italics).

JOZEF ISRAËLS

Printed by BALLANTYNE, HANSON & Co.
Edinburgh & London

9 780469 943247